ETHAN FROME

Edith Wharton

TECHNICAL DIRECTOR Maxwell Krohn
EDITORIAL DIRECTOR Justin Kestler
MANAGING EDITOR Ben Florman

SERIES EDITORS Boomie Aglietti, Justin Kestler
PRODUCTION Christian Lorentzen

WRITERS Jim Cocola, Ross Douthat
EDITORS Sarah Friedberg, Katie Mannheimer

This edition published by Spark Publishing

Spark Publishing
A Division of SparkNotes LLC
120 Fifth Avenue, 8th Floor
New York, NY 10011

Any book purchased without a cover is stolen property, reported as "unsold and destroyed" to the Publisher, who receives no payment for such "stripped books."

02 03 04 05 SN 9 8 7 6 5 4 3 2 1

Please send all comments and questions or report errors to
feedback@sparknotes.com.

Library of Congress information available upon request

Printed and bound in the United States

RRD-C

ISBN 1-58663-422-4

INTRODUCTION: STOPPING TO BUY SPARKNOTES ON A SNOWY EVENING

Whose words these are you *think* you know.
Your paper's due tomorrow, though;
We're glad to see you stopping here
To get some help before you go.

Lost your course? You'll find it here.
Face tests and essays without fear.
Between the words, good grades at stake:
Get great results throughout the year.

Once school bells caused your heart to quake
As teachers circled each mistake.
Use SparkNotes and no longer weep,
Ace every single test you take.

Yes, books are lovely, dark, and deep,
But only what you grasp you keep,
With hours to go before you sleep,
With hours to go before you sleep.

Contents

CONTEXT

E
DITH WHARTON WAS BORN Edith Jones into an upper-class New York City family in 1862. As was typical for members of her class at that time, Edith had a distant relationship with her parents. She received a marriage proposal at a young age, but the wedding was ultimately thwarted by her prospective in-laws' perception of the well-established Jones family's unsurpassed snobbery. In 1885, at the age of twenty-three, Edith married Edward Wharton, an older man whom the Jones family found to be of suitably lofty social rank. At an early stage the marriage turned somewhat sour, but Wharton remained with her husband for well over twenty years. She finally divorced him in 1913, although she never renounced his family name.

The temptations of illicit passion constitute an undeniable focus of Wharton's fiction, and many have pointed to Wharton's unhappy marriage as an explanation. Indeed, Wharton's very success as a writer, so unusual for a woman of her era, may be credited to the fact that her unhappy marriage forced her to devote her energies elsewhere. In fact, Wharton was advised by her doctor to take up the writing of fiction more seriously in order to relieve tension and stress. Eventually, Wharton turned to more tangible sources of relief as well, finding temporary solace in her surreptitious affair with the journalist Morton Fullerton, which coincided with the disintegration of her marriage. It was in the wake of this affair and her ensuing divorce that Wharton wrote many of her most successful and enduring works.

Criticized as an immoral radical in her early years and as a moralizing conservative in her later years, Wharton has been difficult to pin down in her shadowy, shifting beliefs. She was undoubtedly concerned with the moral universe, but, in her fiction, conforming to social norms is constantly at odds with a rejection of conformity. She can perhaps best be described as a critic of moral recklessness, whether this recklessness causes one to lean toward conformity or toward rejection of conformity. Wharton wanted individuals to consider each moral decision on its own terms.

After producing a great quantity of little-read short stories and novels, Wharton enjoyed her first true critical and popular success with the publication of *The House of Mirth* in 1905. In the early 1910s, she settled in Paris, where she remained for the rest of her days. One of her close associates there was the novelist Henry James, a fellow American expatriate of similarly intense and indecipherable moral sensibility.

Ethan Frome, a curious and slender volume first published in 1911, is one of the few pieces of Wharton's fiction that does not take place in an urban, upper-class setting. The novel is all the more remarkable for its austere and penetrating impressions of rural working-class New England, especially given that its author was a woman of leisure, living in the comfort of her Paris salon. Wharton based the narrative of *Ethan Frome* on an accident that had occurred in Lenox, Massachusetts, where she had traveled extensively and had come into contact with one of the victims of the accident. Wharton found the notion of the tragic sledding crash to be irresistible as a potential extended metaphor for the wrongdoings of a secret love affair.

In 1921, Wharton won the Pulitzer Prize for her highly esteemed novel *The Age of Innocence*. She continued to write novels throughout the 1920s, and, in 1934, she wrote her autobiography, *A Backward Glance*. In 1937, after nearly half a century of devotion to the art of fiction, Edith Wharton died in her villa near Paris at the age of seventy-five.

Plot Overview

FINDING HIMSELF LAID UP in the small New England town of Starkfield for the winter, the narrator sets out to learn about the life of a mysterious local named Ethan Frome, who had a tragic accident some twenty years earlier. After questioning various locals with little result, the narrator finally comes to learn the details of Ethan's "smash-up" (as the locals call it) when a violent snowstorm forces the narrator into an overnight stay at the Frome household.

Going back to that tragic year, we find Ethan walking through snowy Starkfield at midnight. He arrives at the village church, where lights in the basement reveal a dance. Ethan loiters by the window, transfixed by the sight of a young girl in a cherry-colored scarf. He has come to the church to fetch his wife's cousin, Mattie Silver, who has been living with the Fromes for over a year, helping around the house. Eventually, we learn that Mattie is the girl in the red scarf—and the object of Ethan's affection.

When the dance lets out, Ethan hangs back to keep his presence unknown. Mattie refuses the offer of a ride from another young man named Denis Eady and begins the walk home alone. Ethan catches up with her. As they continue on their way together, Ethan experiences a sense of thrill in Mattie's presence, and the tension between the two becomes apparent. However, the tension dissipates when they arrive home and Zeena, Ethan's sickly, shrewish wife, who has kept a late-night vigil in anticipation of their return, greets them. She regards the dynamic between her husband and her cousin with obvious suspicion, and Ethan goes to bed in a state of unease, without a word to Zeena and with thoughts only of Mattie.

The next day Ethan spends the morning cutting wood and returns home to find his wife prepared for a journey. She has decided to seek treatment for her illness in a neighboring town, where she will spend the night with some distant relatives. Excited by the prospect of an evening alone with Mattie, Ethan quickly assents to his wife's plan. He goes into town to make a lumber sale, but he hurries so as to return to Mattie in time for supper.

That evening, tensions run high between Ethan and Mattie. Although the two never consummate or even verbalize their passions, their mutual feelings hang palpably between them, unspoiled

3

by the house's many reminders of the absent Zeena. Catastrophe threatens when the cat shatters Zeena's favorite pickle dish, which Mattie had taken out to celebrate their dinner together, but Ethan quickly pieces the shards together and tucks the broken dish back in its place. After supper, with Mattie busy at her sewing work, Ethan contemplates an outright demonstration of his affections, but he stops short of full disclosure. Just after eleven, the two turn in for the night without so much as touching.

The next morning, Ethan remains eager to reveal his feelings to Mattie, but the presence of his hired man, Jotham Powell, coupled with his own inhibitions, prevent him from making a move. Ethan makes a run into town to pick up some glue for the pickle dish. When he arrives back at the farm, expecting to find Mattie alone, she informs him that Zeena has returned. Quickly collecting himself, Ethan visits the bedroom to greet his wife. Zeena, however, is in no mood for kindnesses and bitterly informs Ethan that her health is failing rapidly. In light of this fact, Zeena announces, she plans to replace Mattie with a more efficient hired girl. Ethan privately resents Zeena's decision but keeps the bulk of his anger to himself.

Going down to the kitchen, Ethan's passions spill over, and he kisses Mattie zealously. He tells Mattie of Zeena's plan to dismiss her, but their moment together is interrupted by Zeena herself, who had originally declined to come down to dinner but has changed her mind. After the meal, Zeena discovers the broken pickle dish while in search of some medicines and, in her rage, grows all the more determined to chase Mattie out.

That evening, Ethan retreats to his makeshift study, where he contemplates the decision that lies before him. Unable to tolerate Mattie's dismissal, but effectively unable to prevent it, Ethan briefly considers eloping with Mattie, and even begins to draft a letter of farewell to Zeena. However, in a sober evaluation of his financial situation, Ethan comes to realize the impossibility of running away and falls asleep in a state of hopelessness.

At breakfast the next morning, Zeena announces the day's plans for Mattie's departure and the arrival of the new hired girl. At mid-morning, having finished his tasks on the farm, Ethan steals into town on a desperate errand. His plan, hatched on the fly, is to make a second attempt to collect an advance from Andrew Hale on a recently delivered lumber load, in hopes of financing his elopement with Mattie after all. On his way down the hill Ethan encounters the Hale sleigh, and, in passing, Hale's wife praises him greatly for his patience in caring for the ailing Zeena. Her kind words serve to check his plan, and he returns to the farm with a guilty conscience.

Against Zeena's wishes, Ethan decides to bring Mattie to the station himself. In a fit of nostalgia, he takes her by a roundabout route, and they eventually end up stopping at the crest of a village hill in order to take a sledding adventure they had once proposed but had never undertaken. A successful first run prompts Mattie to suggest a second, but with a different purpose in mind. She asks Ethan to run the sled into the elm tree at the foot of the hill, allowing them to spend their last moments together. Ethan initially rejects her proposal but is slowly won over, and they take their positions on the sled, locking themselves in a final embrace. In the wake of the collision, Ethan comes to consciousness dazedly, reaching out to feel the face of the softly moaning Mattie, who opens her eyes and weakly utters his name.

Jumping forward twenty years, we find ourselves back in the company of the narrator as he enters the Frome household. Inside, he meets the gaze of two frail and aging women, and takes stock of the house's squalid conditions. Frome apologizes for the lack of heat in the house and introduces the narrator to the woman preparing their supper—his wife, Zeena—and to the seated, crippled woman in the chair by the fire—Miss Mattie Silver.

The next day, the narrator returns to town, where he lodges with Mrs. Ned Hale and her mother, Mrs. Varnum. Sensing their curiosity, he gives a brief account of his evening in the Frome household, and after supper he settles down to a more intimate discussion with Mrs. Hale. Together, they mourn the tragic plight of the silent, cursed man and the two women fated to keep him company during the long New England winter nights.

CHARACTER LIST

Ethan Frome The protagonist of the story, Ethan is a farmer whose family has lived and died on the same Massachusetts farm for generations. A sensitive figure, Ethan has a deep, almost mystical appreciation of nature, and he feels a strong connection to the youth, beauty, and vital spirit of Mattie Silver, his wife's cousin. However, he ultimately lacks the inner strength necessary to escape the oppressive forces of convention, climate, and his sickly wife.

Zenobia Frome Ethan's sickly wife, more commonly known as "Zeena." She comes across as prematurely aged, caustic in temperament, prone to alternating fits of silence and rage, and utterly unattractive, making her the novel's least sympathetic figure. She is acutely interested in the treatment of her own illness, displaying a degree of hypochondria (imagined illness or minor symptoms secretly relished and exaggerated by the patient). Despite Zeena's apparent physical weakness, she, not Ethan, holds the dominant position in their household.

Mattie Silver Zeena's cousin, who comes to assist the Fromes with their domestic tasks. Attractive, young, and energetic, Mattie becomes the object of Ethan's affection, and reciprocates his infatuation. Because the reader sees Mattie only through Ethan's own lovesick eyes, Mattie never truly emerges as a well-rounded character. She often seems more a focus for Ethan's rebellion against Zeena and Starkfield than an actual flesh-and-blood person with both strengths and weaknesses.

The Narrator Although he recounts the story's events, the narrator (an engineer by profession) plays no part in the story itself. That he remains nameless highlights the thinness of his character. As a stranger to Starkfield, he views Ethan Frome's story with fresh eyes and operates as a conduit between the closely guarded story of Frome's tragedy and the reader in the world outside the novel.

Denis Eady The son of Starkfield's rich Irish grocer, Michael Eady, and sometime-suitor of Mattie Silver. Denis is the focus of Ethan's jealousy in the novel's early chapters, before Ethan learns of Mattie's true feelings.

Mrs. Ned Hale Widow of Ned Hale and landlady to the unnamed narrator. The narrator describes Mrs. Hale as more refined and educated than most of her neighbors. Although she was once intimate with the Fromes, she hesitates to discuss their plight with her inquisitive lodger.

Ned Hale Ruth Varnum's fiancé and later her husband. Ned and Ruth's romance contrasts with the fruitless love of Ethan and Mattie. Ned has died by the time the narrator comes to Starkfield.

Andrew Hale Ned's father, Andrew Hale is an amiable builder involved in regular business dealings with the young Ethan. When Ethan requests that Hale extend him an advance on a lumber load, Hale is forced to politely refuse, citing his own financial constraints. Nevertheless, Ethan (mistakenly) continues to regard him as a possible source of a loan.

Mrs. Andrew Hale Ned's mother and Andrew's wife, Mrs. Hale extends an unexpected degree of warmth to Ethan after encountering him by chance one winter afternoon. Her kindness and praise for his dedication to Zeena lead Ethan to reevaluate his decision to borrow money from Andrew Hale to elope with Mattie.

Jotham Powell The hired man on the Frome farm. Powell's main duty is to assist Ethan in the cutting, loading, and hauling of lumber. Markedly reticent, Powell is sensitive to the tensions between the Fromes but loath to involve himself in them.

Harmon Gow A former stage-driver and town gossip. Gow provides the narrator with a scattering of details about Ethan Frome's life and later suggests that the narrator hire Ethan as a driver, paving the way for the relationship through which the narrator learns Ethan's story.

ANALYSIS OF MAJOR CHARACTERS

ETHAN FROME

Although the novel's introductory and concluding passages are told from the narrator's point of view, the bulk of the novel unfolds from Ethan Frome's perspective and centers on his actions. Whereas the other characters in the narrative remain opaque, we are allowed access to all of Ethan's thoughts as his life approaches a crisis. He can be seen as the protagonist of the story. In spite of the fact that Ethan contemplates an adulterous affair, Wharton renders him a generally sympathetic character by making extreme efforts to depict his wife, Zeena, as an appallingly unsympathetic figure. Even if we don't condone Ethan's desire for another woman, we understand his motivations. We never doubt his fundamental goodness. Ethan's illicit passion for Mattie Silver coexists with a moral sense strong enough to keep him from going beyond a few embraces and kisses.

Though sympathetic, Ethan remains a frustrating main character. Wharton's novel emphasizes two themes: the conflict between passion and social convention, and the constricting effects that a harsh winter climate can have on the human spirit. These themes almost seem to conspire to make Ethan a passive, unhappy victim of circumstance, weighed down by his duty to his wife, his bitter existence as a poor farmer, and the strain that Starkfield's frozen landscape places on his soul. "Guess he's been in Starkfield too many winters," an old local tells the narrator. This assessment seems to be Wharton's epitaph for her protagonist, who is forced—like the original Ethan Frome and his wife, Endurance, in the graveyard—to endure rather than to act. His entire life becomes a series of dreams destroyed by circumstance. Zeena's illness and his poverty crush his desire for wider horizons, which we see in his hope to leave Starkfield and in his interest in chemistry and engineering. His desire for Mattie is likewise crushed by his inability either to break free of Zeena or to muster the courage to defy convention and risk ruin.

Ethan is a sensitive man, a lover of nature, and a basically decent person, but he lacks emotional strength and so is mastered by circumstances. It is appropriate, then, that his only bold decision in the entire novel is to commit suicide—a decision that Mattie pushes on him and thus, in fact, contains little courage. Rather, his final, mad sled ride to disaster constitutes the ultimate expression of passivity: unable to face the consequences of *any* decision, he elects to attempt to escape *all* decisions forever.

ZENOBIA (ZEENA) FROME

Though Zeena is not as rounded a character as her husband, the negative aspects of her personality emerge quite clearly, making her seem like the novel's villain. While she is technically the victim of Ethan's plans to commit adultery, the reader comes to sympathize much more with Ethan, because he feels imprisoned in his marriage to the sickly and shrewish Zeena.

Wharton's physical descriptions make Zeena seem old and unfeminine. Furthermore, Zeena speaks only in a complaining whine, and all her actions seem calculated to be as vindictive as possible. Her illness might make some of this crotchety behavior forgivable, but she so relishes her role as a sufferer that the reader suspects her of hypochondria, or at least of exaggeration. Her only talent is caring for the sick, and the only time she displays any vitality or sense of purpose is when administering to Ethan and Mattie at the end of the novel. One imagines her taking a perverse delight in Ethan and Mattie's suffering, since she knows that they attempted to kill themselves to escape her. It is important to note, however, that all of Zeena's faults are relayed from Ethan's point of view, which, given his passion for Mattie, is far from impartial.

MATTIE SILVER

Mattie's character constitutes the hinge on which the plot of *Ethan Frome* turns. All of the story's events are set in motion by her presence in the Frome household. Yet we glimpse Mattie, as we glimpse Zeena, only through Ethan's eyes, and his perception of her is skewed by his passion. With her grace, beauty, and vitality, she obviously embodies everything that he feels Zeena has denied him, and so becomes the focus of his aborted rebellion against his unhappy life. Mattie is distinguished by little other than the red decoration she wears, which symbolizes both passion and transgression.

Until the very end, we cannot even be certain that Mattie reciprocates Ethan's feelings for her. When, at the climax of the novel,
Mattie's true self does shine through, we see her as an impulsive,
melodramatic young woman, more adolescent than adult. Her most
active deed of self-definition is persuading Ethan to attempt suicide,
which reveals her as rather immature, ready to give in to whatever
passionate (and foolish) thoughts enter her head. Yet, because the
text has so strongly established Mattie as the horrid Zeena's polar
opposite, we forgive her childish delight in melodrama. Even in her
recklessness, Mattie seems preferable to the shrewish, complaining,
curmudgeonly Zeena: it is better that Ethan die a quick death with
Mattie, we feel, than a slow one with Zeena. Nevertheless, one cannot help but suspect that Mattie may not be quite worth the passion
that Ethan directs her way, and that the rebellion and escape she
represents are more important than the pretty, flighty, and slightly
absentminded girl she actually is.

THEMES, MOTIFS & SYMBOLS

THEMES

Themes are the fundamental and often universal ideas explored in a literary work.

SOCIETY AND MORALITY AS OBSTACLES TO THE FULFILLMENT OF DESIRE

The constraint social and moral concerns place on individual desire is perhaps the novel's most prominent theme, since *Ethan Frome*'s plot is concerned with Ethan's desire for a woman who is not his wife. By denying Zeena a single positive attribute while presenting Mattie as the epitome of glowing, youthful attractiveness, Wharton renders Ethan's desire to cheat on his wife perfectly understandable. The conflict does not stem from within Ethan's own heart—his feelings for Mattie never waver. Instead, the conflict occurs between his passions and the constraints placed on him by society, which control his conscience and impede his fulfillment of his passions.

Again and again, Wharton displays the hold that social convention has on Ethan's desires. Although he has one night alone with Mattie, he cannot help but be reminded of his domestic duties as he sits in his kitchen. He plans to elope and run away to the West, but he cannot bring himself to lie to his neighbors in order to procure the necessary money—and so on. In the end, Ethan opts out of the battle between his desires and social and moral orders. Lacking the courage and strength of will to face down their force, he chooses to abandon life's burdens by abandoning life itself.

WINTER AS A STIFLING FORCE

Ethan Frome, the novel's protagonist, is described by an old man as having "been in Starkfield too many winters." As the story progresses, the reader, and the narrator, begin to understand more deeply the meaning of this statement. Although a wintry mood grips *Ethan Frome* from the beginning—even the name Starkfield conjures images of northern winters—the narrator appreciates the winter's spare loveliness at first. However, he eventually realizes that Starkfield and its inhabitants spend much of each year in what amounts to a state of siege by the elements. The novel suggests that sensitive souls like Ethan become buried emotionally beneath the winter—their resolve and very sense of self sapped by the oppressive power of the six-month-long cold season. Ethan yearns to escape Starkfield; when he was younger, we learn, he hoped to leave his family farm and work as an engineer in a larger town. Though Zeena and poverty are both forces that keep Ethan from fulfilling his dream, the novel again and again positions the climate as a major impediment to both Ethan and his fellow townsfolk. Physical environment is characterized as destiny, and the wintry air of the place seems to have seeped into the Starkfield residents' very bones.

MOTIFS

Motifs are recurring structures, contrasts, or literary devices that can help to develop and inform the text's major themes.

ILLNESS AND DISABILITY

Ethan and those individuals close to him, including (by the end of the novel) Mattie, suffer from sickness or disability. Caring for the sick and the lame defines Ethan's life. He spends the years before the novel begins tending to his ailing mother, and then he has to care for his hypochondriacal wife, Zeena. Finally, after his and Mattie's attempted suicides, Ethan is forced to spend the rest of his days as a cripple, living with a sick wife and the handicapped Mattie. Outward physical signs reflect inner realities in *Ethan Frome,* and the predominance of illness in the characters' physical states indicates that, inwardly, they are all in states of destitution and decline.

SNOW AND COLD

The imagery of *Ethan Frome* is built around cold, ice and snow, and hues of white. The characters constantly complain about the cold, and the climactic scene hinges on the use of a winter sport—sledding—as a means of suicide. These motifs work to emphasize the novel's larger theme of winter as a physically and psychologically stifling force. Like the narrator, we initially find beauty in the drifts, flakes, and icicles. Eventually, however, the unremittingly wintry imagery becomes overwhelming and oppressive, as the overall tone and outlook of the book become increasingly bleak. The cumulative effect is to make the reader feel by the end of the novel that, like Ethan himself, we have "been in Starkfield too many winters."

SYMBOLS

Symbols are objects, characters, figures, or colors used to represent abstract ideas or concepts.

MATTIE'S RED SCARF AND RED RIBBON

In the two key scenes when Mattie and Ethan are alone together— outside the church after the dance and in the Frome house on the evening of Zeena's absence—Wharton emphasizes that Mattie wears red. At the dance she wears a red scarf, and for the evening alone she puts a red ribbon in her hair. Red is the color of blood, ruddiness, good health, and vitality, all of which Mattie has in abundance, and all of which Zeena lacks. In the oppressive white landscape of Starkfield, red stands out, just as Mattie stands out in the oppressive landscape of Ethan's life. Red is also the color of transgression and sin—the trademark color of the devil—especially in New England, where in Puritan times adulterers were forced to wear red A's on their clothes (a punishment immortalized in Nathaniel Hawthorne's *The Scarlet Letter*). Thus, Mattie's scarlet adornments also symbolize her role as Ethan's temptress toward moral transgression.

THE CAT AND THE PICKLE DISH

During their meal alone, and the evening that follows, Ethan and Mattie share the house with the cat, which first breaks Zeena's pickle dish and then seats itself in Zeena's rocking chair. The animal serves as a symbol of Zeena's tacit invisible presence in the house, as a force that comes between Mattie and Ethan, and reminds them of the wife's existence. Meanwhile, the breaking of the dish, Zeena's favorite wedding present, symbolizes the disintegration of the Frome marriage. Zeena's anguish over the broken dish manifests her deeper anguish over her fractured relationship.

THE FINAL SLED RUN

Normally, a sled rider forfeits a considerable amount of control and submits to the forces of gravity and friction but still maintains an ability to steer the sled; Ethan, however, forfeits this ability as well on the final sled run. His decision to coast in his final sled run symbolizes his inability to escape his dilemma through action of any kind. The decision parallels Ethan's agreement to Mattie's death wish, his conduct in his marriage, and his attitude toward life in general: unable to face the consequences of any decision, he lets external circumstances—other individuals, society, convention, financial constraints—make his decisions for him. Mattie's death wish appears especially appealing to Ethan in that it entirely eliminates all consequences for both of them, forever. Just as the rider of a sled relinquishes control, so Ethan surrenders his destiny to the whims of Mattie and of fate.

SUMMARY & ANALYSIS

INTRODUCTION

> *When I had been there a little longer ... I began to*
> *understand why Starkfield emerged from its six*
> *months' siege like a starved garrison capitulating*
> *without quarter.*
>
> (See QUOTATIONS, p. 47)

Due to a carpenters' strike, an engineer (the narrator) spends the winter in the small Massachusetts town of Starkfield, where he comes to learn the tale of Ethan Frome through various sources. The narrator's initial impression of Frome, whom he first encounters at the local post office, is of a silent and unapproachable man with an impressive build and posture. Frome is crippled, and one of his most prominent characteristics is his disfigured face, which was smashed in an accident almost a quarter of a century earlier.

Curious about the details of Frome's accident and about Frome's isolated rural existence, the narrator begins to press some of Starkfield's residents for information. Harmon Gow, a local stagecoach driver, provides a few specifics but fails to understand and convey the deeper meaning of the story. Mrs. Ned Hale, born Ruth Varnum, the middle-aged widow with whom the narrator lodges, proves equally reticent on the subject of Frome.

When the livery stable horses fall ill from a local epidemic, the narrator is left without a way of getting to and from the train station each day for his work. Harmon Gow suggests that the narrator speak with Frome about catching a ride with him. For a week, Frome wordlessly brings the narrator to and from the station each day, a journey that takes nearly an hour each way. One day, after the narrator inadvertently leaves a biochemistry book in Frome's carriage, the two men discover their mutual interest in the field, which leads to a brief interchange on the progress of science. The narrator lends Frome the book in hopes of prompting further conversation, but his hopes prove empty.

A few days later, a driving snowstorm blankets the countryside. The narrator's usual train is delayed, so Frome decides to drive the narrator all the way to his place of business. During the ten-mile journey, they pass Frome's farm, and Frome speaks hesitatingly to the narrator about his changed family fortunes. In silence, they push on through the remainder of the snowstorm, and when they arrive at their destination, the narrator quickly conducts his business before they set out for the return journey to Starkfield. At sunset the storm picks up again, and Frome's horse has trouble keeping to the road in the dark. After a couple of miles of unsure progress, Frome is finally able to identify his gate through the mist and darkness.

The narrator, who has been walking alongside the horse, finds himself completely exhausted, and he suggests to Frome that they have come far enough. Frome agrees, implicitly offering to put him up for the evening. The narrator follows Frome to the barn to settle the horse for the evening, and the two men proceed to Frome's house, a dilapidated building originally constructed in the shape of an L but from which one wing has been removed. In the hallway entrance, Frome shakes the snow from his boots as the voice of a woman drones from within. Frome then opens the inner door to the house and invites the narrator inside. As he speaks, the woman's voice grows still.

ANALYSIS

The narrator's suspicion that the deeper meaning of Ethan Frome's story lies "in the gaps" between scattered details also guides us as readers. Wharton creates an enormous structural gap by beginning the novel near the end of its chronological progression, and the bulk of the novel serves to fill that gap. Because the telling of the tale commences near the conclusion of the drama's events, Wharton is able to lend a tinge of inevitability to the ensuing narrative. The fact that all of the story's events have already happened imbues them with a feeling of finality and fatality, a sense that, just as the events cannot now be altered, they could not then be avoided.

The subtle foreshadowing that Wharton deploys throughout the story may go unnoticed on a first reading, but it plays an instrumental role in the overall conception of this beautiful, tragic romance of Puritan New England. The very name of the town, Starkfield, evokes the bleak mood and rural atmosphere of the story. Images of snow, ice, and cold dominate the descriptive language of the story, forming one of the novel's most important networks of motifs. Paying particularly close attention to the relationship between the landscape and its inhabitants, Wharton emphasizes the way geography shapes human lives. She paints Frome as an "incarnation" of the silent, melancholy, and frozen countryside. Frome's cold demeanor is the emotional reflection of his physical environment.

Although it would be a mistake to identify *Ethan Frome*'s narrator as Edith Wharton herself, there is little evidence from which to shape a profile of the narrator as an individual wholly separate from Wharton. We may assume the narrator to be male, since, at the turn of the twentieth century, a woman would be unlikely to be involved in interstate business travel and even less likely to interact so casually with virtual strangers in a small-town environment. Nevertheless, the narrator never reveals his name nor, explicitly, his gender. By creating an unknown outsider to lead us into the story, Wharton is able to create further psychological distance between the reader and the already withdrawn Frome. To see the importance of this device, one need only imagine how different the story would be were it presented from the perspective of a local Starkfield resident.

The narrator's perspective obtrudes little over the course of the book. The tone of most of the novel is one of detached omniscience—the narrator gives us Frome's story as he (the narrator) has understood it after having gathered all of the facts. However, in this introductory section, the narrator asserts the limited nature of his understanding as he first became acquainted with Frome's story, and the reader therefore receives a more subjective impression of Frome and his surroundings.

From the outset, the narrator found Frome "the most striking" resident of Starkfield as well as "the ruin of a man." Frome's imposing nature owes in part to his grotesque crippled body and stiff face, which are the result of the briefly mentioned "smash-up" on which much of the story's mystery rests. Frome's farmhouse is symbolic of his own dilapidated state. Like its owner, the house has fallen on hard times and lost its original shape, and the narrator notes that he saw "in the diminished dwelling the image of [Frome's] own shrunken body."

Although the narrator notes Frome to be reserved and isolated, some of his interaction with the recluse reveals that Frome may not always have displayed such lack of passion and spirit. When he speaks briefly to the narrator about a trip he once took to Florida and about his former interest in the sciences, we see a hint of Frome as he once was. Additionally, despite his reticent nature, Frome proves willing to help the narrator when needed, and his offer to drive the ten miles up and back to the junction in a heavy snowstorm clearly exceeds the narrator's expectations. But just as the narrator prepares to enter Frome's house, we, as readers at the mercy of Wharton's shifts in perspective, are left behind at the doorstep, left to take the longer road to understanding, which winds all the way back to the beginning of Frome's story.

CHAPTER I

SUMMARY

At midnight, through an accumulated snowfall of some two feet, a young Ethan Frome walks the quiet streets of Starkfield. Near the edge of the village, he stops in front of the community church, where a dance is being held. He makes his way around the church's perimeter and settles in front of a basement window, craning his neck to get a view of the festivities. The dance is concluding, and the assembled group is preparing to leave. But when the young, handsome, and energetic Denis Eady jumps back onto the dance floor and claps his hands, the musicians take up their instruments and the dance hall again fills with life.

Ethan focuses his attention on Mattie Silver, a girl wearing a cherry-colored scarf and dancing with Eady. She is cousin to Ethan's wife, Zeena, and has been living with the Fromes as a housekeeper for over a year. Ethan, who has come to walk Mattie home from the dance, has become quite attached to her in the course of the year, finding a kinship with her in their mutual appreciation of nature. As he watches her whirling effortlessly among the pulsating crowd, he wonders why he had ever dreamed that the feelings of attraction might be mutual. It seems to him that her free and easy movement between partners indicates her indifference toward him.

Ethan recalls a recent conversation with Zeena, in which she suggested that Mattie might marry Denis Eady and that they would need to hire a new girl to help—"the doctor don't want I should be left without anybody," she insists. This memory disquiets him, and as he waits for Mattie, he begins to brood.

ANALYSIS

Beginning with Chapter I, Wharton plunges the reader into the story with a jolt of energy that is quite different from the more conversational tone of the narrator's frame. The description of Starkfield at midnight, with the excited dancers whirling indoors while the world outside lies frozen, overflows with sensory details. Moreover, the warmth and richness of the scene inside the church creates a strong impression of the young Ethan as a man set apart from society. Married prematurely to an ailing, unattractive wife, Ethan feels despair at his exclusion from the revelry. Yet, he also takes a certain pleasure in his position as an unnoticed voyeur.

While the sensory richness of the first scene bursts suddenly into the mind of the reader, Wharton reveals factual information at a much more gradual pace. She tempers the scandal by composing it piecemeal, through a slow, subtle process of accumulated information, which keeps our minds open to the narrator's own descriptions and analysis. At the outset, the young Ethan's reason for gazing through the church window is unclear. We see that he is infatuated with a girl in a cherry-colored scarf, but his romantic interest only gains significance once Wharton discloses that Ethan is already a married man and that the object of his desire is his own wife's cousin, who lives under his own roof. In light of these details, Ethan's preoccupation with Mattie Silver takes on an illicit air.

Wharton presents and describes Denis Eady and Mattie Silver before giving them names or dialogue of their own. This approach achieves a certain realism, as we must observe these characters and make inferences about them, just as we would with new acquaintances in real life. Mattie, in particular, becomes burned into the reader's consciousness through the focus of Ethan's own consciousness—her twisting, fluttering, cherry-colored scarf. Brightly colored and shining vividly amid the matte, wintry landscape, the scarf marks Mattie as a person worthy of notice (her last name—Silver—likewise suggests that she flashes like metal and is therefore highly visible). The scarf's redness, symbolizing devilishness or sin, suggests that Mattie may be a figure of wrongdoing or rebellion. As the plot unfolds, she does indeed come to embody transgression against social convention in the name of individual passions, a notion that takes on thematic import in the novel as a whole.

CHAPTER II

SUMMARY

> *Against the dark background of the kitchen she stood*
> *up tall and angular, one hand drawing a quilted*
> *counterpane to her flat breast, while the other held*
> *a lamp.* (See QUOTATIONS, p. 48)

As the dance ends, Ethan first hears and then sees Mattie emerge, but he shrinks back in the shadows to avoid initiating contact. The crowd thins out rapidly, and Mattie is left wondering what has kept Ethan from coming to meet her. As Mattie stands alone, Eady approaches, offering to take her for a ride in his father's cutter (a light sleigh drawn by a horse). Ethan, still hanging back, observes Mattie seeming to waver, and wonders whether she will go with Eady or refuse his attentions. After unhitching the horse from its post and setting the cutter in motion, Eady confidently calls out to Mattie to hop in. She politely declines. When Eady attempts to pick her up by linking arms with her, she draws away gracefully. As Frome listens to the bells of the cutter fade away in the distance, he sees Mattie's shadow walking alone up the hill toward the silent snow bank.

Ethan quickly closes in on Mattie, surprising her with his presence when he catches up to her amidst the Varnums' spruce trees. She is genuinely caught off guard by his trick and lets out a peal of laughter that thrills Ethan. They link arms together and look at the "coasting hill," where people go sledding. Ethan says they can sled there the following night if the moon is out. Mattie mentions that Ned Hale and Ruth Varnum, a young engaged couple, nearly collided with the big elm at the bottom of the hill when they were sledding. "We were all sure they were killed," she says with a shudder.

Beginning the hike home, Ethan continues to wonder about Mattie's feelings toward Eady and decides to press the issue by needling Mattie about her behavior at the dance. But his roundabout fashion of pursuing the conversation only leads Mattie to believe that Ethan's wife, Zeena, is on the verge of dismissing her. Mattie wonders if Ethan himself is similarly inclined, although dismissal of Mattie is the furthest thing from Ethan's mind. Left at an impasse, the couple drops the subject wordlessly, and Ethan and Mattie continue on their way.

At the Frome gate, Ethan attempts to reassure Mattie, and the companions then draw together as they ascend the hill. Ethan, meditating on the prospect of being with Mattie always, puts his arm decidedly around her for the first time. At the back door of the dark house, Ethan searches for the key that Zeena usually leaves out for them, but he finds nothing. When Ethan kneels down for a more thorough search, he spies a faint ray of light behind the door. The door then opens to reveal Zeena, a sickly, complaining woman. Zeena explains that she was unable to sleep on account of her poor health, and she brings her lamp around to the stairs to light the way up. Ethan declares that he will be staying downstairs for a while, as he has some accounts to review. When Zeena dismisses the idea as a foolish one, he submissively follows her and Mattie upstairs, retiring into the bedroom with his wife.

ANALYSIS

In Mattie, Ethan finds a somewhat mystical kinship—the text compares Ethan's infatuation with his wife's cousin to the "shock of silent joy" that he feels when he contemplates the beauties of nature. Given his sensitivity to place, it is no surprise that Ethan feels especially energized during his nighttime walks home from town with Mattie. During these moments, Ethan feels most strongly the "sweetness" of the connection between them.

Standing between Ethan and Mattie is the ailing Zeena, another character whom Wharton reveals only by hints and degrees. An early passage describes Zeena as having sharp and suspicious eyes, and although the conversation that Ethan remembers as he stands outside the church (summarized in the previous section) seems harmless, Zeena's words resonate with hidden insight. For instance, when Zeena states to Ethan that the doctor thinks she shouldn't be left alone, it seems that she is arguing the necessity of a housekeeper, but underlying this remark is Zeena's sense that Ethan and Mattie could run off together. Just when we are sure that Zeena's sole concern is the possibility of Mattie leaving, she makes a caustic remark about the fact that since Mattie's arrival, Ethan has taken to shaving every day. This remark also seems to belie Zeena's well-founded suspicion of an intrigue between her husband and her cousin, as does her evening vigil.

Wharton's caricature-like depiction of Zeena makes her seem like an old woman who possesses neither beauty nor kindness. Jux-

taposed with Mattie, Zeena serves as a foil (a character whose atti-
tudes or emotions contrast with and thereby accentuate those of
another character), highlighting Mattie's vigor. Mattie seems to
embody health, with her vibrant scarf and her last name, Silver,
which suggests brightness. Zeena, on the other hand, speaks in a
"flat whine," and when she appears at the doorway to greet Ethan,
Wharton dwells on her "flat breast," "puckered throat," and the
"hollows and prominences" of her face. The contest for Ethan's
heart is no contest at all—Mattie seems to be Ethan's soul-mate,
Zeena a nagging, hypochondriacal shrew.

Because the reader already knows, by the time the narrator meets
Ethan, that Ethan is crippled, a mood of foreboding hangs over the
story. The "throng of disregarded hints and menaces" that crowd
Ethan's mind at the dance foreshadows the impending danger. The
conversation about the sledding hill, with its mention of the poten-
tially deadly elm, also constitutes a deliberate and obvious foreshadowing of later events.

Chapter III

Summary
The morning after the dance, Ethan heads out early to the wood lot
to attend to some hauling. He and Zeena have not exchanged a single word since retiring the previous night, during which Ethan lay
awake for many hours, preoccupied by his thoughts of Mattie. As
he hauls the wood, Ethan regrets that he didn't kiss Mattie when
they were alone together the night before.

Ethan's mind then turns to the relationship between Mattie and
Zeena, which has been chilly ever since Mattie came to live in Starkfield, after her father died. A sense of dread and foreboding fills
Ethan, and he channels his fear by throwing himself into his work
until midday. He considers driving his lumber load into the village
at once, but then thinks better of it and returns to the house to check
on the women. Coming in, he is surprised to see Zeena sitting at the
table in her best dress, with a small piece of luggage at her side. She
says that she cannot stand her recurring pains any longer and has
resolved to set out for Bettsbridge on an overnight visit in order to
see a new doctor. Ethan quickly agrees to Zeena's proposal that
Jotham Powell, the hired man, drive her to the train station. He
would drive her himself, he says, but he must collect a direct cash

payment from Andrew Hale upon his delivery of a load of wood that afternoon. Ethan's excuse is a lie, since Hale is unlikely to pay up, but Ethan has no desire to go for a long ride with his wife.

ANALYSIS

As Ethan toils at his farm work, his thoughts of Mattie stream into a series of worries that reveal his capacity as a "seer," one who senses the subtle signs of looming tragedy. Ethan's thoughts also tell us about the nature of the tragic events to come, so that we too become seer[s] of a sort. Wharton associates Ethan's insights into the future with his ability to predict rain, despite appearances to the contrary on "stainless" mornings. We can perceive that this statement is a metaphor for the state of Ethan and Mattie's relationship: although Ethan's conduct with Mattie has hitherto remained stainless, from our knowledge of his desire for her, we can predict the "storm" that they will soon experience. Ethan's reaction to his foresight is a passive denial. As he grows increasingly aware of an inevitable disaster surrounding his passion for Mattie, he throws himself into his logging with extra zeal, as though hard work will enable him to escape from what we already understand to be predestined.

As Ethan muses on his present love for Mattie, the narrator muses on Ethan's loveless marriage, undertaken out of fear of misery rather than true devotion. The moment introduces one of the novel's themes: the conflict between warm inner desire and cold external realities. The theme receives emphasis when, in subsequent chapters, we learn of Ethan's dream to leave his farm and work in a town—perhaps even as an engineer—and see how circumstances conspire to thwart him.

Again and again, Wharton links Starkfield's weather to the characters' emotional states to show that the external world takes precedence over the internal landscape of a character's being. No description in the novel is neutral. We learn that the bleakness of the New England winters contributed to the sense of loneliness and depression that pushed Ethan into Zeena's sickly arms: the marriage between Ethan and Zeena might not have happened if Ethan's mother "had died in spring instead of winter." Every setting seems to restrict, inhibit, and debilitate, generating sickness and disability—another of the novel's themes. By this point in the novel, we have learned of Ethan's mother's illness, of Zeena's maladies, and of the disabilities that Ethan suffers by the end of the story's plot.

Zeena's unexpected departure for Bettsbridge can be seen as evidence of either naïveté or mistrust. Certainly, departure is the last move that one would expect of a suspicious wife. For this reason, Ethan assumes—logically, but perhaps foolishly—that Zeena must truly need medical attention. A more skeptical interpreter of Zeena's trip might consider it a clever attempt to learn the true nature of Ethan's feelings for Mattie by putting those feelings to the test. Whatever the case, Ethan seems unable even to suspect his wife of having an ulterior motive. Ethan's attitude toward his wife lacks subtlety, as does Wharton's portrayal of Zeena as an ugly shrew. Neither the author nor Ethan seems to have any sympathy for Zeena, and, consequently, neither do we. Zeena exists not as a complicated character but as a stumbling block to Ethan's happiness with Mattie.

CHAPTER IV

SUMMARY

As soon as Jotham and Zeena set out for Bettsbridge, Ethan departs to deliver the lumber load to Andrew Hale. During his journey, he is consumed by thoughts of his return to Mattie, imagining their first night alone together. After recounting these thoughts, the narrator segues smoothly into a description of the circumstances that surrounded Ethan's courtship of Zeena and their subsequent marriage. When Zeena came to help Ethan nurse his mother, her arrival made him feel less lonely. Fearing the return of his loneliness when his mother died, Ethan asked Zeena to marry him. He had originally planned to sell the farm and move to a larger town, but Zeena's illness soon rendered his dream impossible.

Since he mentioned to Zeena that he would be receiving cash for the lumber load, Ethan decides to go ahead and ask Andrew Hale for a small direct payment. After unloading the lumber, Hale invites Ethan into his office, and Ethan requests an advance of fifty dollars. Hale politely refuses, citing his own financial constraints, and after a further exchange of civilities, Ethan leaves Hale to conduct some other business in the village.

With the afternoon drawing to a close, the street stands relatively empty. After an interval of solitude, a swiftly moving horse-drawn sleigh carrying Denis Eady passes Ethan and heads in the direction of the Frome farm. Ethan feels a fleeting pang of jealousy, which he quickly suppresses as unworthy of his affections for Mattie. Under the cover of the Varnum spruces, Ethan happens upon Ned Hale and Ruth Varnum, locked together in a clandestine embrace. Realizing that they are being watched, the kissing couple quickly separates and departs. Ethan is left to reminisce about the scene, which, he notes, has taken place in the very spot where he and Mattie stood hesitating the previous night.

Ethan makes the long climb back to the farm. When he arrives, he looks up to see a light issuing from Mattie's bedroom. He imagines her preparing herself for supper, and he thinks back to the evening of her arrival, when she had taken such care with her appearance. On his way to the house, Ethan passes a gravestone that he has often considered a curiosity. It marks the resting place of one of his ancestors, also named Ethan Frome, as well as that of the ancestor's wife, who was named Endurance. They DWELLED TOGETHER IN PEACE FOR FIFTY YEARS, the stone announces. Ethan wonders if the same words will be written about him and Zeena.

Arriving home, Ethan finds the door locked. Mattie opens it, in her usual dress but with a streak of crimson ribbon in her hair. She has carefully set the supper table for Ethan with festive treats and colorful serving dishes. After Ethan removes his outerwear, he returns to the kitchen, where Mattie has put the teakettle on the table. She playfully admits to entertaining Jotham Powell over a cup of coffee, which makes Ethan prickle slightly with jealousy. At supper, the cat jumps up onto the table, upsetting and breaking a pickle dish. The accident drives Mattie to tears, because Zeena had forbidden her ever to use the dish, a favorite wedding present of Zeena's that came all the way from Philadelphia. Ethan confidently consoles her, balancing the fragments into a convincing whole high atop the closet, where it would be unlikely that Zeena could detect the breakage. Having averted the disaster, Ethan and Mattie settle back down at the table to finish their supper.

ANALYSIS

Ethan's silent fascination with the gravestone outside his house displays the extent to which his life is permeated by the severe, Puritan notion that all human action is predetermined. As he stares at the gravestone, which memorializes the lives and fifty-year marriage of

ETHAN FROME AND ENDURANCE HIS WIFE, Ethan believes his own fate is spelled out before him. The former Frome's wife's name seems to embody Ethan's own situation: he no longer lives life but merely endures. Although Ethan fully recognizes the obstacle that Zeena poses to his happiness, he refuses to act to rectify the situation.

Although Ethan believes that the course of his own marriage is fated by the marriage of his ancestor, the narrative plays upon the relationship between past and present within Ethan's own life. When Ethan attempts to rebel against his situation, his feelings for Mattie develop in a curious replay of his earlier courtship of Zeena. First, Ethan felt he needed Zeena, a family cousin who came to care for his mother. Now, Ethan finds himself falling for Mattie, a family cousin who has come to care for his wife. The narrative plays upon this parallel when Ethan comes home from his business transaction to find the porch door locked, just as he did the previous night— only this time it is Mattie and not Zeena who comes to the door.

The illusion of a man-and-wife evening is set into motion but with a difference, symbolized by the crimson ribbon in Mattie's hair. In its coloring, the ribbon refers back to the daring cherry-colored scarf that Mattie wears at the dance hall. It alludes to the scarlet letter that Hester Prynne wears to symbolize her transgression in Nathaniel Hawthorne's classic Puritan novel *The Scarlet Letter.*

When the couple sits down to dinner, Wharton begins to describe the nooks and crannies of social artifice. The festive, rather impulsive-seeming, and sexually symbolic dishes Mattie has prepared— blueberries, pickles, doughnuts—indicate Mattie's awareness of the evening's clearly illicit nature. Nevertheless, Ethan and Mattie conduct the opening motions of their first supper alone with all of the elaborate gestures and rituals that might occur in the most fashionable cosmopolitan salon. Their stiff formality is shattered—literally—when the cat breaks Zeena's favorite wedding present, symbolizing the way that Mattie may break up Zeena and Ethan's marriage. Ethan's response to the broken dish is also symbolic. Rather than securing the shattered dish permanently with glue or simply throwing away the pieces and admitting that the dish has been broken, Ethan arranges the fragments into a delicate balance, postponing disaster. The dish, and his marriage, appear unbroken, but they may in fact fall to pieces with the slightest disturbance.

CHAPTERS V–VI

SUMMARY: CHAPTER V

> *Now, in the warm lamplit room, with all its ancient*
> *implications of conformity and order, she seemed*
> *infinitely farther away from him and more*
> *unapproachable.* (See QUOTATIONS, p. 49)

After supper, Mattie clears up while Ethan takes a last turn around the yard. He returns to the kitchen to find Mattie busy at her sewing. Taking up his pipe, he sits down contentedly by the stove. When Ethan calls Mattie in to join him, she sits in Zeena's rocking chair, and Ethan suddenly imagines the specter of Zeena's face to have appeared in place of Mattie's features. Perhaps sensing her companion's unease and feeling uneasy herself, Mattie returns to her station in the kitchen. In time, Ethan and Mattie's disquiet begins to melt away, and they begin a carefree conversation about everyday matters—including, once again, the possibility of going sledding on the next moonlit night. However, when Ethan brings up his sighting of Ned and Ruth kissing among the spruces, Mattie suddenly becomes silent.

Once again, Ethan and Mattie find themselves avoiding the subject that is on both of their minds—their relationship. Ethan discusses Mattie's marriage prospects, and Mattie discusses Zeena's ill will toward her. Dismissing the subject of Zeena, they fall silent again, until Ethan boldly places his hand on the opposite end of the piece of cloth on which Mattie is working. Mattie, in recognition of this gesture, ceases her activity and waits.

The stillness is interrupted by a clatter. Behind Ethan and Mattie, the cat has leapt from Zeena's rocking chair in pursuit of a stray mouse. This sudden reminder of Zeena oppresses Ethan, and he impulsively picks up his end of Mattie's sewing work and kisses it gently. As he does so, the fabric slips from his hold, and he looks up to see Mattie putting away her sewing kit for the evening. The clock strikes eleven. Mattie asks about the fire, and after straightening up the room, she lights a candle and blows out the lamp. As she prepares to climb the stairs, Ethan says goodnight to her, and she responds in kind. Ethan, hearing the door to her room pull shut, realizes that he has not even touched Mattie's hand during the course of the evening.

Summary: Chapter vi

At breakfast the following morning, Jotham Powell sits between Ethan and Mattie. Overnight, the wet snow has turned to sleet, creating poor road conditions and giving the men cause to load the remaining lumber at once, but delay their last actual haul until the afternoon. When Powell heads out to harness up the horses, Ethan and Mattie are left alone again, and Ethan has an urge to say, "We shall never be alone again like this." He stifles it, however, and settles for telling her that he will be home for dinner.

In town, after unloading the lumber, Ethan heads to the Eady store in search of some glue to fix Zeena's broken dish, but he can't find any there. Ethan then hastily goes to the widow Homan's store, where, after a lengthy search, he finally finds a single bottle of glue. In a driving rain, Ethan pushes his team of horses furiously toward home. When he arrives, he puts them away without a thought and dashes into the kitchen.

Ethan triumphantly announces to Mattie that he has obtained the glue, but his excitement quickly dissipates when Mattie whispers that Zeena has returned—she has headed upstairs to her room without so much as a word to Mattie. Out at the barn, while Ethan feeds the horses, Powell returns to put away the sleigh. Ethan invites him to stay for supper, but Powell declines. His refusal throws Ethan into a fit of unease, and he is filled with foreboding as he goes back inside, where Mattie tells him that dinner is ready.

Analysis: Chapters v-vi

In the midst of Ethan and Mattie's unspoken feelings for one another, Zeena seems almost supernaturally present. For example, when Mattie vacates Zeena's chair uneasily, it continues to rock for a few moments, as though Zeena has reoccupied it. The mischievous cat seems to represent its absent owner, doing everything in its power to remind Mattie and Ethan of their obligations to Zeena. The cat creates general chaos by hopping up into Zeena's seat at supper and upsetting the pickle dish; later, as if to solidify its role as Zeena's ambassador, the cat jumps up into her place and watches the would-be couple with suspicious eyes. Ethan himself introduces Zeena into the room when, as Mattie sits in Zeena's rocking chair, he mentally transposes Zeena's face onto Mattie's body. This act reveals Ethan's subconscious desires and fears—although he wishes for Mattie to assume a marital role with him, he also lives in anguished torment with regard to the consequences, which embody themselves fully in the fearful appearance of Zeena's ghostly visage.

In the close confines of the familiar, lived-in room, Ethan feels trapped and paralyzed by a realm of conventions in which Mattie seems infinitely out of reach. His home carries associations of conformity, convention, and moral order, which stunt his and Mattie's conversation. This stilted conversation contrasts sharply with the free-flowing, easy conversation Ethan and Mattie enjoyed the evening before, during their nighttime walk. Ethan's attempt to overcome his shyness is, in a sense, conducted for its own sake, in revolt against the societal strictures that limit him. In the unshakable silence, Ethan's shy kiss of Mattie's sewing work is a strictly symbolic gesture, a desperate attempt to act on his emotions—to prove to himself that he is capable of doing so. When Mattie blushes at the mention of Ruth and Ned as lovers, she acknowledges the sexual tension between herself and Ethan, yet she too feels powerless to take any real action.

The subject of sledding is raised a second time in Chapter V, and again it is associated with death. "There's an ugly corner down by the big elm," Ethan says. "If a fellow didn't keep his eyes open he'd go plumb into it." This assessment is foreshadowing with a vengeance, since the story ends with Mattie and Ethan sledding into that same tree, and Wharton almost seems to be hammering the reader over the head with the information.

Jotham Powell's presence at breakfast in the morning tempers the tension between Ethan and Mattie. Not only is Jotham another body in the room, but, as Ethan's hired hand, Jotham symbolizes the workaday world that stands between Ethan and his dream. Significantly, during Ethan's village journey of the previous afternoon, it is Powell, not Denis Eady, who visits Mattie after delivering Zeena to her train. Eady has been positioned several times as a possible obstacle to a union between Mattie and Ethan, but the true obstacle is not some intrigue on Mattie's part, but the everyday world. If Mattie is unreachable, the reason is not, as Ethan fantasizes, Denis Eady.

Powell's neutralizing presence, so unwanted during Zeena's absence, suddenly becomes desirable to Ethan after his wife's return. For this reason, Ethan extends a dinner invitation to Powell, hoping to diffuse the tension between him and the two women. Powell's puzzlingly abrupt refusal adds an air of impending disaster to the upcoming meal. The total change in the household's atmosphere is further registered when Mattie speaks again: her simple statement that she supposes it is time for supper bears an entirely different set of nuances than the same words held only twenty-four hours before.

CHAPTER VII

SUMMARY

> *For a moment such a flame of hate rose in him that it ran down his arm and clenched his fist against her. He took a wild step forward and then stopped.*
>
> *"You're—you're not coming down?" he said in a bewildered voice.* (See QUOTATIONS, p. 50)

After hanging up his coat, Ethan calls to Zeena but receives no reply. He goes up the stairs and opens her door, revealing a nearly dark room. Still wearing her traveling clothes, Zeena sits silently at the window. When Ethan informs her that supper is ready, she says she has no appetite. Zeena cuts short Ethan's attempts to make small talk by announcing that she is much more ill than he thinks. She tells him that in the interest of preserving her health, she has engaged the services of a new hired girl, who will arrive the following afternoon.

Ethan becomes angry at this unforeseen expense, and a raging war of words ensues between him and Zeena. After a bitter haggle regarding Zeena's condition, in which she insists that she lost her health nursing his mother, Ethan resolutely declares that he lacks the funds to employ a hired girl. But, in so doing, he is caught in his own lie about the advance he had been planning to collect from Andrew Hale. When Zeena points out Ethan's inconsistency, he is somewhat shaken. Zeena then further agitates Ethan by announcing that Mattie has burdened the household for too long and will have to leave. With Mattie's board freed up, Zeena explains, they will be able to scrape together enough money for a hired girl after all.

Just at that moment, Mattie calls up from the landing to announce that supper is waiting. Zeena replies by declining her supper, and Ethan sends Mattie downstairs, promising to follow shortly. Turning back to Zeena, Ethan lamely attempts to defend Mattie. Zeena refuses to listen, proclaiming that with the hired girl's arrival, Mattie must depart. Ethan fumes with hatred, but he stops himself from expressing it. Instead, he retreats from the bedroom as Zeena prepares to lie down for the night.

In the kitchen, Mattie brings a meat pie to the table, and she and Ethan once again sit down to supper alone. Ethan assures Mattie that everything is fine, but his disgust makes him unable to eat, and his dark mood produces a new wave of anxiety in Mattie. As she questions Ethan further, he rises from his seat and moves around the table to her side. With a trembling perplexity, Mattie leans toward him. As if to resolve matters, Ethan takes her into his arms and kisses her fully upon the lips. She remains in his grasp for a moment and then draws back to make sense of the situation.

With a violent outburst, Ethan declares that Mattie must not go. Confused at first, Mattie soon catches his meaning and realizes that Zeena intends for her to be replaced. After sitting in silence for a while, they forlornly begin to discuss Mattie's bleak prospects for future employment. Filled with indignation, Ethan exclaims that he means to protect Mattie from dismissal and expulsion. No sooner have the rebellious words erupted than Mattie raises her hand in warning—Zeena comes in and quietly takes her seat at the table between Ethan and Mattie. Citing her need for nourishment despite her lack of appetite, Zeena starts eating her meal. Ethan sits motionless and Mattie attempts to make polite conversation. The cat rubs up against Zeena, and she strokes it and feeds it a scrap of meat.

After finishing her meal, Zeena rises from the table to find some old stomach powders. Mattie begins clearing the table, and Ethan muses that he will go outside to watch the nightfall. At the door, he meets an indignant Zeena on the verge of tears, holding the shards of the pickle dish in her hand and demanding an explanation. When pressed, Ethan blames the accident on the cat. Rushing to Ethan's defense, Mattie explains that she had taken the pickle dish down to decorate the supper table. Zeena reprimands Mattie for her sneakiness and declares that she should have turned her out long ago.

ANALYSIS

The increasing gravity of Zeena's illness—or at least what she *claims* is the increasing gravity of her illness—invests her with a ruthless authority in these scenes. Wharton compares Zeena's discussions of her sickness with the behavior of someone chosen for "a great fate." Zeena doesn't see her ailment as a curse; she acts as though her ability to live with suffering proves her "elect" status, her virtue, and fortitude. She casts herself as a noble martyr, telling

Ethan that although anyone else would need an operation given her condition, she is willing to struggle on without one.

Zeena's placement of herself in the role of a martyr is certainly Ethan's greatest obstacle in his attempt to keep Mattie, but even without Zeena claiming the higher moral ground, Ethan would be out of his depth. Zeena calls the shots because Mattie is her relative, not Ethan's. Likewise, the domestic realm is Zeena's concern, not Ethan's. Zeena's dominance within the household becomes obvious when Ethan, seething, has a sudden urge to strike at her but then inexplicably reverts to a state of passive bewilderment and meekness, retreating downstairs. Similarly, Zeena's well-timed entrance into the kitchen forces Ethan back into silence just as he has finally managed to reveal his true feelings to Mattie.

Certainly, Ethan realizes that Zeena, a chronic hypochondriac, is exaggerating the severity of her illness in order to gain the upper hand in their relationship. Nevertheless, he remains powerless to oppose her. The self-possessed Zeena so carefully crafts her statements that, though they may be lies, Ethan cannot disprove them. Ethan, on the other hand, lacks grace and articulateness. He clumsily allows Zeena to catch him in his own lie about the lumber advance, and then proves unable to cover his tracks. As Wharton squarely notes, Ethan is no good at lying, and his natural streak of honesty is a factor in his eventual inability to realize his own dreams.

The broken pickle dish that Zeena discovers at the top of the china closet symbolizes the shattered Frome marriage. Mattie is partially responsible for the breaking of both the pickle dish and the marriage, having handled them carelessly, and Ethan cowardly hides the broken state of each. Significantly, though, it was the cat that actually destroyed the dish. Throughout the narrative, the cat is associated with Zeena, so the cat's destruction of the pickle dish suggests that Zeena must share responsibility for the failure of her marriage. Zeena uses the dish as an excuse to vent anger that in fact stems from the disintegration of the relationships around her. She mourns for the destruction of the dish because she cannot openly mourn the collapse of her marriage and happiness.

Meanwhile, the reader is left uncertain of Mattie's feelings, because Zeena's arrival cuts short Mattie's conversation with Ethan after he kisses her. We assume that she feels the same passion that Ethan does, but her words do not betray anything. Instead of discussing the kiss, she immediately turns the conversation to Zeena and the possibility of her own departure from the household.

CHAPTER VIII

SUMMARY

Directly following her outburst over the broken dish, Zeena retires upstairs to bed, and a shaken Mattie continues to clear up the kitchen. Ethan makes his usual rounds outside the house and returns to find the kitchen empty. His tobacco pouch and pipe have been laid out on the table next to a brief note in Mattie's handwriting telling him not to worry. Retreating into his makeshift study, Ethan contemplates the note over and over again, pondering a way out of his unbearable situation.

Flinging aside in disgust a handmade cushion of Zeena's, Ethan mentally reviews the case of a local man who had deserted his wife in favor of the woman he loved. Encouraged by this precedent, Ethan resolves to run away with Mattie, and he prepares to write a letter of farewell to Zeena, leaving her the farm and the mill. But Ethan pauses at the prospect of starting over without any money, and he pictures the grim situation in which Zeena will be left. Slowly, he comes to the bitter recognition of his plan's impracticality, and he crumples back to the sofa in tears, falling asleep beneath the light of a large moon in the beautiful winter night sky.

Ethan wakes up cold, stiff, and hungry, and rises in the knowledge that this will be Mattie's last day beneath his roof. As he stands alone in his study, he hears a step behind him and turns around to see Mattie, full of concern for his well-being after having listened all night for his return upstairs. Ethan, overwhelmed by her show of caring, lights the kitchen fire for her, and, as they sit down to a breakfast of leftovers, they decide not to worry about Zeena's threats. Ethan heads out to the cow barn, where he encounters Powell. When Powell presses to secure the details for the new hired girl's arrival and Mattie's departure, Ethan responds by saying that the matter of Mattie's dismissal is itself still unresolved. Powell reacts indifferently to this piece of news.

Back in the kitchen, the men enter to find Mattie and Zeena seated at a full breakfast table. Zeena eats heartily, feeds scraps to the cat, and discusses departure and arrival times with Powell. She then endeavors to settle a few final matters with Mattie, as Ethan looks on wordlessly.

After finishing his morning tasks, Ethan tells Powell that he is heading into town and that they should not wait for him to have dinner. Frantically searching for a solution, Ethan decides again to ask Andrew Hale for the advance on the lumber, feeling that Hale would relent if he thought that the money would make a difference in Zeena's health. With the money, Ethan decides, he will be able to run away with Mattie and start a new life elsewhere. Aiming to intercept Hale before he departs for work, Ethan runs quickly down the hill, and spots the Hale wagon in the distance. Arriving at its side, he finds not Hale but Hale's wife in the sleigh. She informs him that Hale is resting at home for the morning, and she speaks kindly to him about his fortitude in caring for Zeena before she goes on.

Mrs. Hale's compassionate words encourage Ethan in his errand: if the Hales feel so sympathetic toward him, he thinks, surely they will advance him the cash. But after a few paces, Ethan's conscience catches up with his fantasies, and he realizes the extent of the deception in which he is prepared to engage. With his ethics now gaining dominance over his passions, Ethan slowly turns around and heads back to the farm.

ANALYSIS

Ethan's defining characteristic in this chapter is indecision. He desperately wants to abandon Zeena but lacks the courage to do so, and he tries to convince himself that it is not his wife but financial reality that is holding him back. The novel evokes the image of a prison contracting around him: "The inexorable facts closed in on him like prison-warders hand-cuffing a convict. There was no way out—none." The phrase bears much truth: in many ways Ethan is indeed a prisoner of circumstances beyond his control. Still, a tinge of melodrama flavors his insistence that there is "no way out"; it seems that if he *really* wanted to elope with Mattie, he could manage it. Admittedly, such a decision would present financial difficulties, but one senses that Ethan's cowardice and obedience to social mores, as well as his personal ethics, constitute the real forces that keep him from eloping. He uses money matters to justify his decision not to run away to the part of himself that wants to do so.

As we question the sincerity of Ethan's financial worries, we also question how realistic his assessment of his and Mattie's relationship may actually be. Mattie's behavior clearly demonstrates that she has feelings for Ethan, but Ethan seems to be making a large leap when he imagines her going out west with him; after all, they have shared only one kiss so far. Mattie remains more of an ideal to him, one senses, than a reality; he loves her for herself, but also because she represents an opportunity for "rebellion" against the twin tyrannies of custom and geography, which tie him to his hypochondriac wife and his snowbound farm. She is the "one ray of light," he thinks, in the darkness of his prison, and his terror over losing her seems to be a terror at the prospect of seeing, like the Ethan Frome on the gravestone, fifty years with Zeena consume his time on earth.

Until now the snowy landscape has symbolized Ethan's spiritual oppression, with the recurring wintry imagery serving as a reminder of his status as a prisoner of Starkfield. On the morning of Mattie's departure, however, the landscape is transformed: there is sunlight and "a pale haze of spring" over the snow, so that the wintry fields seem to hold a promise of renewal and rebirth. This promise, of course, Ethan associates with Mattie, and Wharton draws an obvious parallel between Mattie's shining last name, Silver, and the sudden beauty adopted by nature: "the fields lay like a silver shield under the sun. . . . Every yard of the road was alive with Mattie's presence." Again the text emphasizes Frome's mystical connection to the natural world, as he sees the events of his own life reflected in the beauty around him.

Meanwhile, Ethan's plans continue to oscillate wildly. At night, in his study, he gives in to despair; the next day, the sun and the hint of spring seem to revive him, and he begins to plan for escape again. Yet, once again, his fears and his sense of conscience overcome him, as the unexpected kind words of Mrs. Hale are enough to thwart his temporary determination to escape from Starkfield. The theme of personal desires being repressed in favor of social order recurs here: Ethan cannot get the money that he needs from the Hales, because to do so would be to violate the complex web of duty and obligation that defines the community of Starkfield. He wants to rebel, but he cannot bring himself to do what is necessary to bring that rebellion to fruition.

CHAPTER IX

SUMMARY
Arriving back home, where a sleigh has come to take away Mattie's trunk, Ethan enters the kitchen to find Zeena reading a book of medical advice. When he asks about Mattie, Zeena tells him that she is upstairs packing. Ethan climbs the stairs and enters her room,

finding Mattie sitting on her trunk in the middle of the emptied room, sobbing. She confesses her fear that she will never see him again. He reassures her, pulling her close to him and placing his lips on her hair. They are interrupted by Zeena, who calls for the trunk to be hurried down. Ethan carries it downstairs to the sleigh, and as he and Mattie watch the horse and rider depart, Ethan resolves that he, not Powell, will drive Mattie to the train.

At dinner, Ethan is unable to touch his food, while Zeena eats heartily. After the meal, Powell asks what time he should return to deliver Mattie. Ethan explains that he won't need to come to the farm at all, as Ethan himself will be delivering Mattie to the station. This sudden change of plans does not sit well with Zeena, who tells Ethan that he needs to attend to the stove in the spare bedroom. A bitter exchange ensues, and Ethan firmly insists on taking Mattie in spite of Zeena's protests.

Filled with nostalgia and regret, Ethan prepares his horse for the journey. Returning to the house, he finds the kitchen empty; he eventually locates Mattie in his old study, where she explains that she had wanted to take one last look around. Zeena has retired to her bedroom after dinner without a single word of goodbye to Mattie. After casting one last glance around the kitchen, Mattie is ready to join Ethan, entering the sleigh and starting down the hill.

Ethan decides to take Mattie the long way around, along Shadow Pond, in order to relive a handful of memories. Ethan stops the sleigh in a pine wood and helps Mattie down. As they walk together through the wintry landscape, they remember their encounter of the previous summer at a church picnic on this very spot, where Ethan found a lost gold locket of Mattie's. Lingering in the glow of their reminiscence, Ethan longs to reach out to Mattie and declare his affections openly, but she rises to go before he can make his move.

They drive on under a setting sun, and Ethan asks Mattie about her plans for the future. She outlines a vague notion of finding work in a store. Ethan declares his devotion to her, and she responds by showing him his aborted letter of goodbye to Zeena, which he had left in his study and which Mattie had then found. Ethan is exhilarated by her discovery and asks if she has the same feelings for him that he does for her. In despair, she dismisses his question as useless, tearing up the note and casting the fragments into the snow. However, moments later, she quietly confesses her own love for him.

Ethan explains the impossibility of his situation, and Mattie insists that he write to her. Worried that she will eventually marry,

Ethan asserts that he would almost sooner see her dead, and Mattie tearfully agrees with his sentiment. As they drive, they come across a group of boys with sleds, which reminds them of their long-harbored plan to go sledding. Suddenly, Ethan proposes that they embark on their sledding adventure right away, reassuring Mattie that the hired girl can wait for them at the station. Sighting a sled beneath the Varnum spruces, they make their way over to it and climb aboard.

They finish their first run smoothly, though they narrowly miss the elm that stands at the foot of the first slope. As they climb back up the hill together, Ethan is struck with the thought that these are their last moments in each other's company. At the top of the hill, Mattie breathlessly asks Ethan if this was the same place where he once saw Ned Hale and Ruth Varnum kiss each other, and she embraces him in a kiss of their own. As they say their goodbyes—still refusing to accept them as goodbyes—and kiss again, the church clock strikes five. Unable to bear the prospect of parting from Ethan, Mattie solemnly requests that Ethan steer the sled so they coast directly into the elm tree and die together. Ethan's initial astonishment quickly gives way to his own desire to escape a future without Mattie. Locked in a lover's embrace once again, Ethan holds Mattie close and feels her sobbing, as the train whistle sounds.

The two pile onto the sled together, with Ethan sitting in front, and Ethan sets the sled into its fatal motion. As they hurtle down the hill, Ethan feels confident that they will hit the tree, but at the last moment he swerves unexpectedly, as he seems to see Zeena's malignant face before him. The sled glides off in a second of uncertainty before he rights it on its course again. They then hit the elm.

Ethan, dazed from the impact, hears the faint noises of what he takes to be a small animal in pain, and he makes a weakened effort to attend to it. After removing a heavy mass from on top of him, he reaches out to feel what he discovers to be Mattie's hair and face. Rising to his knees, he bends down toward Mattie's face, seeing her eyes open and hearing her utter his name. He moans softly back to her. Hearing his horse whinny at the top of the hill, he is brought back to the world and the duties that face him there.

ANALYSIS
From the beginning of this chapter the sense of despair and desperation begins to mount, with time running out for Ethan and Mattie.

In this somber mood, the sense of unavoidable doom grows, and the narrative builds up to its dramatic climax. In his emotional strain, Ethan finds himself seemingly guided by the invisible force of destiny: Wharton describes him feeling as though his heart were tied with cords being tightened by the hand of fate. Due to this "unseen hand," Ethan relinquishes responsibility for his own actions, pursuing his errand with Mattie as though directed by a greater force. In a heartbeat, Ethan's notions of ethical responsibility have dissipated, and his entire sense of accountability vanishes along with it.

The dynamics between Mattie and Ethan change subtly now as Mattie, for the first time in the book, seizes the initiative in their interactions: she takes the bold step of revealing her knowledge of Ethan's forsaken plan to elope with her and the even bolder step of confessing her own longtime love for Ethan. Yet the declaration brings no real happiness: now that we know that Ethan's passion is not one-sided, Mattie's imminent departure takes on an infinitely more tragic dimension. At the same time, Mattie's daring seems to bring out a dangerously reckless quality in Ethan, as he gives in to a sudden impulse and proposes the sledding adventure.

In light of the book's final circumstances, Ethan's inner thoughts in this scene create a sense of bitter irony. Poised at the top of the hill for their first run, Ethan's playful reassurance to Mattie that he could go down the hill with his eyes closed foreshadows their impending deliberate crash. Moreover, Ethan's wish to keep Mattie with him forever will attain a terrible form of realization when Mattie is crippled in the ensuing crash and forced to stay with the Fromes indefinitely. Similarly, Ethan's thought that their ascent up the hill will be the last time they walk together also bears a grave dramatic irony: they will never walk together again, as it turns out, not because Mattie is leaving him, but because she will soon be unable to walk at all.

Part of the genius of *Ethan Frome* is the way that the sledding run works as a metaphor for Ethan's inability to make the decisions necessary to solve his dilemma. Sledding is an activity in which the rider submits to the forces of gravity and friction: a certain amount of steering can alter the course, and some riders steer better than others, but the rider can always choose to give in to momentum and simply coast. Giving in is exactly what Ethan does in agreeing to Mattie's suicidal wish: he frees himself of the burdens of his situation and makes the decision to coast, putting his life and hers in the hands of fate. In many ways, this notion of coasting also applies to

Ethan's general approach to life: believing himself to be imprisoned by external contingencies—by the landscape, financial circumstances, and social conventions—he relinquishes responsibility time and again.

So, too, does the sledding run fit perfectly with the nature of Ethan and Mattie's love, which is illicit and reckless, and so seems to call for a reckless conclusion. This ending feels destined to the characters as well as to the reader: in considering Mattie's death wish, Ethan reflects that Mattie seems to be speaking for fate itself. It is as though he has no other choice but to comply with her bold proposal. In keeping with his mystical outlook, Ethan comes to believe that the natural world around him has somehow sanctioned their decision: as the sled hurtles violently toward the elm, Ethan observes that the elm seems to be waiting for them, as though it knows what will happen.

But the sledding run, as it turns out, is not an escape of any kind. Wharton leaves it ambiguous whether Ethan's swerve, brought about by his vision of Zeena, is what prevents them from dying or whether even a head-on collision is not enough to kill them. In either case, the world has conspired to prevent Ethan and Mattie from escaping, and now the book's dominant themes reemerge as strongly as ever: the conflict between human desires and the external circumstances, be they geographical or social.

Wharton had provided the first foreshadowing of the smash-up at the outset of the story, when the narrator heard vague descriptions of Ethan's unfortunate accident from several reluctant village sources. Combined with the later references to sledding accidents, Ethan's pronounced disfigurement in the opening pages of the novel clues the reader in to Ethan's impending tragedy. Nevertheless, the grip of Wharton's rustic romance is so strong as to fog the memory of even the most perceptive first-time readers; we read of the disaster in near disbelief, and no amount of preparation seems adequate to dampen the emotional impact of the literal collision.

SUMMARY & ANALYSIS

CONCLUSION

SUMMARY

> *I don't see's there's much difference between the*
> *Fromes up at the farm and the Fromes down in the*
> *graveyard; 'cept that down there they're all quiet, and*
> *the women have got to hold their tongues.*
>
> (See QUOTATIONS, p. 51)

Entering Frome's kitchen, the narrator is unable to tell which of
the two women in the room had been speaking upon the men's
arrival. Both are slight and gray-haired, and one starts preparing
the evening meal as the other sits huddled in the corner by the
stove. The narrator observes the marked poverty and squalor of the
place, and Frome notes the coldness of the room with a tone of
apology. The woman in the corner attempts to explain, blaming
the other woman for having only just started the fire. The
narrator then recognizes the whining voice he heard previously as
the voice of the seated woman. As the other woman comes back
around to the table to set a pie in place, Frome introduces her to the
narrator as his wife and then proceeds to introduce the seated
woman as Miss Mattie Silver.

The next morning, the narrator returns to his lodgings, to the
great relief of Mrs. Hale, who had given him up for dead. Mrs. Hale
and her mother, Mrs. Varnum, are most surprised to learn of
Frome's exceeding generosity toward the narrator, and they react
with downright amazement at his announcement that he has spent
the night at the Frome household. The narrator senses a strong hint
of curiosity in the two women regarding Frome's hospitality. Mrs.
Hale submits that she has spent a great deal of time visiting the
Fromes, but for the last twenty years hardly anyone but herself and
their doctors has ever set foot in the household.

After supper, Mrs. Varnum retires for the evening, and Mrs. Hale
and the narrator sit in the parlor for a further conversation about the
Fromes. Mrs. Hale begins to recount the terrible aftermath of the
smash-up, but the mere memory of Mattie's convalescence suffices
to bring her to tears. Gathering her wits, Mrs. Hale continues with
her tale, describing to the narrator Zeena's mysteriously silent reaction to the events and her gracious decision to receive Mattie back
into their household as soon as she could be moved.

Responding to the narrator's gentle queries, Mrs. Hale explains that Mattie has lived with the Fromes ever since and that Zeena has done much of the caretaking for the three of them. Expressing pity for them and marveling at their resilience, Mrs. Hale seems to have concluded her account; however, she then collects herself to make one final remark. Removing her spectacles and leaning toward the narrator in confidence, she declares in a lowered voice that Mattie would have been better off dying after the accident, for, as it stands, "I don't see's there's much difference between the Fromes up at the farm and the Fromes down in the graveyard; 'cept that down there they're all quiet, and the women have got to hold their tongues."

ANALYSIS

In this brief epilogue, Wharton summons us back to the present, resuming the narrator's description of his visit to the Frome household. The result is an abrupt and curtailed view of Frome's plight, of which we now hold a background understanding. As she did in the novel's opening scenes, Wharton once again delays the revelation of character, describing the individuals at hand before she names them. From the neutral narrator's description, it is initially difficult to tell which woman is which, and when we hear that one speaks in a "whine," the word Wharton uses earlier to describe Zeena's voice, we assume that this complainer is Zeena—only to realize, with a trace of horror, that the voice belongs to Mattie.

Thus, everything comes full circle, and the cyclical nature of life on the farm is embodied in the terrible fate of Ethan and the women. Instead of finding escape in suicide, he and Mattie have ended up in a state of living death, in which all Mattie's vitality has been leeched away, and she has transformed into a carbon copy of her former opposite, Zeena. Zeena herself, appropriately enough, has been restored to greater health by the necessity of caring for her crippled husband and cousin—as if she can be healthy only when others suffer. Certain aspects of the characters have remained constant throughout. Always quiet and inscrutable, Zeena remains impossible to interpret, and the reader is left ignorant of her opinions about the situation. "Nobody knows Zeena's thoughts," Mrs. Hale says, and the text confirms that her "pale opaque eyes . . . revealed nothing and reflected nothing." Nonetheless, one can imagine her taking a kind of perverse delight in the failure of Ethan and Mattie's attempt to escape her, as well as in the brutal justice of their fate.

Once again we witness the recurrence of the theme of physical surroundings as destiny. Ethan, Zeena, and Mattie all have become trapped—by snow and poverty and their disabilities—in the decaying farmhouse, and they will be trapped there forever, as Mrs. Hale's closing words remind us: they will join the other Fromes in the graveyard, alongside the headstone of the earlier Ethan Frome and his wife, Endurance. And indeed, for Ethan himself, endurance is all that remains: his attempt at rebellion and escape has failed, and he ends where he began, trapped by illness, poverty, and winter in Starkfield, waiting for death.

Important Quotations Explained

1. When I had been there a little longer, and had seen
    this phase of crystal clearness followed by long
    stretches of sunless cold; when the storms of February
    had pitched their white tents about the devoted village
    and the wild cavalry of March winds had charged
    down to their support; I began to understand why
    Starkfield emerged from its six months' siege like a
    starved garrison capitulating without quarter.

This quotation is from the introduction, in which the narrator describes his experience of a Starkfield winter. His metaphorical comparison of Starkfield's struggle against the harsh winter and a "starved garrison" struggling against a besieging army establishes one of *Ethan Frome*'s principal themes: the bleak, harsh physical environment surrounding the characters acts as an oppressive power, forcing a sort of spiritual surrender and emotional listlessness. When one of the old inhabitants of Starkfield says that Ethan Frome has "been in Starkfield too many winters," he means that Ethan has lived for too long in what amounts to a state of siege by the climate. The novel suggests that when snow buries Starkfield each year, the emotions, dreams, and initiative of sensitive souls like Ethan also become buried, destroyed by the "long stretches of sunless cold."

2.   Against the dark background of the kitchen she stood
     up tall and angular, one hand drawing a quilted
     counterpane to her flat breast, while the other held a
     lamp. The light . . . drew out of the darkness her
     puckered throat and the projecting wrist of the hand
     that clutched the quilt, and deepened fantastically the
     hollows and prominences of her high-boned face
     under its rings of crimping-pins.

This quotation, from the end of Chapter II, is the strongest physical
description that we have of Zeena Frome, and it is not a flattering
one. The phrases combine to support a picture of Ethan's wife as
unfeminine, dried-up, overly thin, and generally unappealing.
Female beauty is traditionally associated with curves and images of
fertility, yet Zeena is all hard angles and protruding bones—with
her flat breast and tall figure, she seems stripped of all sexuality, all
romantic allure. Moreover, she appears very *old*. Her aged features
bespeak her inner weariness as well as her demand for respect and
her lack of playfulness. Her unattractiveness and premature aged-
ness contribute to the novel's sharp opposition between Zeena and
Mattie: Zeena Frome is cold and unappealing, a woman prone to
long silences, who is always described as speaking in a "flat whine,"
while Mattie Silver is a picture of youthful vigor and beauty, with a
sparkling personality and name to match. In the contest for Ethan's
devotions, all that Zeena has on her side is convention and her husband's inertia. Ultimately, however, these prove enough to prevent
Ethan from fulfilling his dreams and passions.

The language of this passage evokes not only ugliness and aged-
ness, but also sickness and death. Zeena's thinness may result in
part from her chronic illness. Moreover, when the narrative draws
attention to the "fantastically" exaggerated "hollows and prominences" in her face, its "ring of crimping-pins," it is evoking more
than mere ugliness: it conjures the picture of a skull, with its gaping
eye sockets and its streamlined silhouette of a head. Thus, not only
does Zeena represent coldness in opposition to robust sexuality and
fertility; here she is the picture of death itself, in opposition to life in
general. With her, the description implies, day-to-day existence is
nothing more than a living death. Escape from her and her household is thus more than a question of indulging a whim; it may indeed
be a matter of spiritual survival.

3.   He knew that most young men made nothing at all of
       giving a pretty girl a kiss, and he remembered that the
       night before, when he had put his arm about Mattie,
       she had not resisted. But that had been out-of-doors,
       under the open irresponsible night. Now, in the warm
       lamplit room, with all its ancient implications of
       conformity and order, she seemed infinitely farther
       away from him and more unapproachable.

This quote sums up Ethan's state of mind in the middle of Chapter
v, when Zeena is away and he is alone in the house with Mattie. It
touches on one of the themes of the work—namely, the conflict
between desire and social or moral order—as the warm living room,
with all its reminders of marital obligation and traditional ethics,
makes Mattie seem infinitely out of reach.

The previous night, Ethan reflects, circumstances had seemed
different, but then he was out in the "open irresponsible night." The
indoors embodies the opposite force, the force of responsibility and
duty, which literally walls Ethan in and prevents him from acting on
his passion for Mattie. The outdoors, in contrast, represents the setting where both Ethan and Mattie seem most in their element: elsewhere in the book, both appreciate the beauties of the snow and
woods, and they appear to enjoy an almost mystical connection
with nature.

Yet the forces represented by the indoors ultimately prove to be
more powerful: Ethan is a man of conscience, and he cannot bring
himself to violate the dictates of his society's moral order. Furthermore, because he is forced to choose between desire and convention
in his living room of all places, his choice is almost predestined: he
cannot give in to rebellion in this place, with its reminders of everything that the moral order is supposed to protect—namely, the
hearth and home.

QUOTATIONS

4.   All the long misery of his baffled past, of his youth of
       failure, hardship and vain effort, rose up in his soul in
       bitterness and seemed to take shape before him in the
       woman who at every turn had barred his way. She
       had taken everything else from him; and now she
       meant to take the one thing that made up for all the
       others. For a moment such a flame of hate rose in him
       that it ran down his arm and clenched his fist against
       her. He took a wild step forward and then stopped.
          "You're—you're not coming down?" he said in a
       bewildered voice.

This passage from Chapter VII makes clear that Ethan is a physically
strong man, but, as the reader comes to understand over the course
of the novel, he lacks force of personality. Zeena has just announced
her intention to expel Mattie from the house; Ethan's consequent
fury achieves such heights that a definitive outburst between him
and his wife now seems inevitable. His clenched fist even hints at
potential physical violence. Yet these emotions ultimately lead
nowhere, as his fury dissipates into a "bewildered voice," a sharp
contrast to his inner "flame of hate." Ethan may be filled with emotional turmoil, but he ultimately proves weaker than his wife; she
can impose her will upon him as she likes, and he cannot muster the
boldness necessary to oppose her.

   For this reason, *Ethan Frome* is in many ways a story of inaction,
of an affair that *doesn't* happen. Ethan's only proactive move is his
attempted suicide, which is more an expression of cowardice than of
true courage. Ethan sees Zeena as the cause of his thwarted dreams
and recurring failures, believing them to "take shape before him" in
the figure of his wife. In many ways, Zeena is indeed responsible for
much of Ethan's suffering: shrewd, calculating, manipulative, and
domineering, she exerts an active control over her husband. Yet
Ethan may also prove too eager to place the blame entirely on his
wife: Zeena becomes more of an excuse for his inaction than its
real cause.

5.   There was one day, about a week after the accident,
     when they all thought Mattie couldn't live. Well, I say
     it's a pity she *did* . . . if [Mattie] ha' died, Ethan might
     ha' lived; and the way they are now, I don't see's
     there's much difference between the Fromes up at the
     farm and the Fromes down in the graveyard; 'cept that
     down there they're all quiet, and the women have got
     to hold their tongues.

These words, the last lines of *Ethan Frome,* are spoken by Mrs. Hale
as she discusses the state of affairs in the Frome household since the
sledding disaster. Her comment seals the mood of brutal despair
permeating the conclusion, as we realize the full horror of Ethan's
life. He is trapped not only with Zeena but with a Mattie who has
been transformed into a crippled copy of his wife, in a dilapidated
farmhouse buried under a perpetual winter. The comparison
between the Fromes' life and the corpses' existence in the graveyard
emphasizes certain aspects of Ethan's fate: it underlines the perma-
nence of his situation, implying that his imprisonment is irreversi-
ble, like death.

The allusion to the gravestone is the second in the book: the first
reference comes in the form of a detailed description of the stone
and Ethan's reaction to it. There, we learn that the stone marks the
graves of one Ethan Frome and his wife, named Endurance. Recall-
ing this information, we realize that for Ethan himself, endurance is
all that remains, now that his attempt at rebellion has failed.

Although Mrs. Hale speaks of Ethan as if he had died ("if [Mat-
tie] ha' died, Ethan might ha' lived"), she is of course implying that
he has in fact met a worse fate—that he is experiencing death in life.
Indeed, if there is one thing more fearsome than death, it is a living
death: with bitter irony Mrs. Hale points out that the women in the
graveyard at least hold their tongues, implicitly contrasting this
silence to the whining that fills the Frome household. With this
observation, then, she forces one last tragic realization: while there
may seem to be little difference between corporeal death and living
death, actual death contains the benefit of peace, of a final state of
rest. A living death—Ethan's tragic fate—continues to torment the
soul for years.

KEY FACTS

FULL TITLE
Ethan Frome

AUTHOR
Edith Wharton

TYPE OF WORK
Novel

GENRE
Tragic romance

LANGUAGE
English

TIME AND PLACE WRITTEN
1910, in Paris

DATE OF FIRST PUBLICATION
1911

PUBLISHER
Scribner's, New York

NARRATOR
An anonymous visitor to Starkfield, Massachusetts, narrates the introduction and conclusion. In Chapters I–IV, the story flashes back approximately twenty years to Ethan Frome's youth and the first-person narration gives way to a limited third-person narration (predominantly reflecting Ethan Frome's point of view).

POINT OF VIEW
The frame story (introduction and conclusion) is told in the first person, from the narrator's limited point of view as a visitor unfamiliar with Starkfield and Ethan Frome. However, most of the book is written in the third person limited, in which the narrator accesses Ethan's thoughts but not those of the other characters.

TONE
Foreboding, bleak, ironic, tragic, spare

TENSE
Past

SETTING (TIME)
The late nineteenth–early twentieth century

SETTING (PLACE)
Starkfield, Massachusetts

PROTAGONIST
Ethan Frome

MAJOR CONFLICT
Ethan's main fight is with his own conscience, as he decides
whether or not to reveal to Mattie his true feelings. His struggles
are exacerbated by his surroundings—Zeena, the bleak
Starkfield landscape, his home—which often take on an
oppressive quality.

RISING ACTION
Ethan's passion for Mattie grows as he walks her home from a
dance; Zeena goes away for the night, leaving Ethan and Mattie
alone, but they find their dinner together tense and awkward;
Zeena decides to replace Mattie with another household helper;
Ethan drives Mattie to the train station and neither can stand to
leave the other.

CLIMAX
Ethan and Mattie confess their love for each other and decide to
commit suicide by sledding into a large tree.

FALLING ACTION
Ethan and Mattie regain consciousness after crashing into
the elm; Zeena takes both of them in and cares for them into
old age.

THEMES
Society and morality as obstacles to the fulfillment of desire;
winter as a stifling force

MOTIFS
Illness and disability; snow and cold

SYMBOLS
Mattie's red scarf and red ribbon; Zeena's cat; Zeena's pickle
dish; the final sled run

FORESHADOWING

The repeated references to sledding, and to the dangers associated with it, foreshadow the climactic scene in which Ethan and Mattie crash into the elm. The narrator's introduction to the story describes Ethan as a crippled man who has had an accident, foreshadowing that his relationship with Mattie will meet a tragic end.

STUDY QUESTIONS & ESSAY TOPICS

STUDY QUESTIONS

1. *How does Wharton use symbolism to reinforce plot development in* Ethan Frome?

The course of events in *Ethan Frome* is punctuated by a series of obvious symbolic devices, each of which serves to illustrate the development of the relationships among Ethan, Mattie, and Zeena. First, we encounter the connection between Mattie and the color red—she wears a red scarf to the dance and a red ribbon in her hair for her dinner alone with Ethan. In both cases, the color symbolizes her vitality and attractiveness in contrast with Zeena's cold demeanor. It also symbolizes her temptation of Ethan toward sexual transgression. The cat that disrupts Ethan and Mattie's meal and breaks Zeena's favorite dish symbolizes the wife's dominating spiritual presence in the Frome household, and how she comes between her husband and her cousin in their budding romance. Finally, Ethan and Mattie's climactic sled ride symbolizes the careening, out-of-control course that Ethan embraces when he sets prudence aside and gives in to Mattie's impulsive death wish. The sled ride is also symbolic of his more general approach to life—he relinquishes responsibility and agency and surrenders to momentum.

Thus, each of Ethan's and Mattie's three critical scenes together—outside the church, alone at home, and on the sledding hill—is marked by patent symbolism on Wharton's part. Because by interpreting the symbols we add meaning to Ethan and Mattie's interaction that neither of the characters perceives, Wharton's use of symbolism creates dramatic irony. Along with the narrator's use of foreshadowing, the dramatic irony created through symbolism adds to the sense of inevitable doom that surrounds the novel's events.

2.   *Is Ethan a strong person? Why or why not?*

When the narrator first comes to Starkfield, he is struck by the "careless powerful look" that Ethan Frome possesses in spite of his crippled body. Clearly, Ethan possesses great *physical* strength, which coexists with a strong, well-formed conscience—he is undeniably a good person. Nevertheless, he seems to lack inner strength; his story stands as an illustration of the way that a person can be mastered by, rather than a master of, circumstances. He fails to realize any of his desires, and although one can hardly blame him for it, one feels that Ethan must nevertheless bear some responsibility— for allowing Zeena's illness to crush his desire to leave Starkfield, and then for never daring to break with convention and with his wife in the name of his romantic passions. The only proactive deed he undertakes is the final sled ride. Yet even this has been pushed on him by Mattie—and suicide represents what is ultimately only a continued passivity. Unable to face the consequences of any actual decision, Ethan lets Mattie make a choice for him; and although his is the deed that seals that choice, it is a choice to end all choices.

3. *Discuss the relationship between the physical environment of Starkfield and the nature of the characters' inner states.*

Not only does bleak, oppressive cold shape Starkfield's physical landscape; it penetrates the characters' psychic landscapes as well. Early on, the narrator uses a metaphor of a city under siege to describe Starkfield in winter, comparing the freezing, snowy weather to a besieging army, and the inhabitants of Starkfield to a "starved garrison." This metaphor establishes the theme of how Starkfield's icy climate oppresses human lives. Just as the village's spirit is crushed by the six months of ice and snow, so Ethan's personal spirit is crushed—an old man describes Ethan as having "been in Starkfield too many winters." Ethan's home comes to seem like a prison that constricts him.

Wharton emphasizes that Ethan yearns to escape Starkfield. Before Zeena's illness, he had planned to sell his farm, move to a larger town, and find work as an engineer. But he never escapes, and the reader has the sense that the oppressive spirit of the endless winters, along with his poverty and Zeena's illness, seem to have settled over his heart, pinning him to one place. Mattie, with her high spirits and red trimmings—which contrast sharply with the deathly whiteness of Starkfield—appears to offer Ethan a way out, but in the end she, too, succumbs to the aura of the landscape. By the end of the novel, we see her sitting in the Frome farmhouse during a blizzard, complaining bitterly about the cold.

Suggested Essay Topics

1. What does the presence of the unnamed "narrator" in the story's introduction and conclusion contribute to the effect of the novel?

2. Discuss the novel's portrayal of Zeena. Does her harshness seem realistic?

3. Examine the significance of the gravestone of ETHAN FROME AND ENDURANCE HIS WIFE. How does it relate to the novel's themes?

4. How does Wharton's use of Ethan's point of view to portray Mattie influence our perception of the girl? What does Wharton seem to think of her? Consider the Introduction and Conclusion along with the rest of the novel.

5. In your opinion, do Ethan, Mattie, and Zeena deserve their fates? Does the story aim to teach its readers a lesson? Which aspects of the novel make us sympathize with the characters, and which aspects seem to ask us to pass negative judgment?

REVIEW & RESOURCES

QUIZ

1. What is the name of Ethan Frome's hometown?

   A. Starkfield
   B. Boston
   C. Deerfield
   D. Snowtown

2. With whom does the narrator lodge?

   A. Mattie Silver
   B. Zenobia Frome
   C. Mrs. Ned Hale
   D. Harmon Gow

3. What brings the narrator to Ethan Frome's house?

   A. His desire to buy the Frome farm
   B. A snowstorm
   C. Labor negotiations
   D. A search for a missing girl

4. Who does Ethan wait for outside the church hall?

   A. Zeena
   B. The narrator
   C. Ruth Varnum
   D. Mattie Silver

5. What is taking place in the church hall?

   A. A dance
   B. A church service
   C. A political meeting
   D. A funeral

6. Which young man has an obvious romantic interest in Mattie?

    A. Andrew Hale
    B. Jotham Powell
    C. Denis Eady
    D. Ned Varnum

7. What color is the scarf that Mattie wears at the dance?

    A. Blue
    B. Red
    C. Green
    D. Silver

8. In what season does *Ethan Frome* take place?

    A. Spring
    B. Summer
    C. Fall
    D. Winter

9. What is the name of Ethan's wife?

    A. Zeena
    B. Ruth
    C. Mattie
    D. He is unmarried

10. Why does Zeena decide to go away for a night?

    A. She wants to visit her relatives
    B. She needs to have an operation
    C. She wants to see a doctor in a neighboring town
    D. She has a job interview in another town

11. How did Ethan come to marry his wife?

    A. He met her at a church social
    B. She came to nurse his mother, and he proposed to her
    C. He met her while on a tour of duty in France
    D. The marriage was arranged by their fathers

12. What does Mattie make for dinner when she and Ethan are alone?

    A. Peas and stewed meat
    B. Pasta
    C. Corn and potatoes
    D. Pickles and doughnuts

13. Who breaks Zeena's favorite dish?

    A. The cat
    B. Mattie
    C. Ethan
    D. Jotham Powell

14. What name is on the gravestone that Ethan often looks at?

    A. Ezekiel Frome
    B. Nathaniel Hawthorne
    C. Ethan From
    D. Zenobia Frome

15. What do Ethan and Mattie do when they are alone together at night?

    A. They kiss
    B. They talk uncomfortably and never touch
    C. They poison the cat
    D. They profess their mutual love

16. What does Ethan buy in town in Chapter VI?

    A. A new dress for Mattie
    B. Flowers for Zeena
    C. Lumber
    D. Glue to fix the broken dish

17. When Zeena returns, what does she tell Ethan?

    A. That she is divorcing him
    B. That she has hired a new girl to work in their house
    C. That she knows Ethan and Mattie are having an affair
    D. That she loves Ethan dearly and is sorry for her past coldness

18. What is Zeena's plan for coming up with more money?

    A. She suggests that Ethan take another job
    B. She expects an inheritance
    C. She wants to cease harboring Mattie in their home
    D. She wants Mattie to take a job in town

19. What does Zeena discover after supper on the day of her return from Bettsbridge?

    A. Her broken pickle dish
    B. The cat's dead body
    C. Ethan and Mattie kissing
    D. Dishes left unwashed from the previous night

20. Who does Zeena want to drive Mattie to the train?

    A. Ethan
    B. Mattie herself
    C. Ned Hale
    D. Jotham Powell

21. Who actually drives Mattie to the train?

    A. Jotham Powell
    B. Ethan
    C. Zeena
    D. Ruth Varnum

22. From whom does Ethan plan to get money in order to elope with Mattie?

    A. His parents
    B. Zeena
    C. Andrew Hale
    D. Jotham Powell

23. What do Mattie and Ethan do together before her train arrives?

    A. They go sledding
    B. They chop wood
    C. They poison Zeena
    D. They visit the graveyard

24. What does Mattie convince Ethan to do at the end of Chapter IX?

    A.   Elope with her
    B.   Divorce Zeena
    C.   Move to Hawaii
    D.   Commit suicide with her by sledding into a tree

25. Whom does the narrator find in Ethan's house?

    A.   Jotham Powell
    B.   Two dead bodies
    C.   Mattie, now married to Ethan
    D.   Zeena and a crippled Mattie

ANSWER KEY:
1: A; 2: C; 3: B; 4: D; 5: A; 6: C; 7: B; 8: D; 9: A; 10: C;
11: B; 12: D; 13: A; 14: C; 15: B; 16: D; 17: B; 18: C; 19: A;
20: D; 21: B; 22: C; 23: A; 24: D; 25: D

SUGGESTIONS FOR FURTHER READING

BELL, MILLICENT, ed. *The Cambridge Companion to Edith Wharton.* New York: Cambridge University Press, 1995.

BLOOM, HAROLD, ed. *Edith Wharton.* New York: Chelsea House, 1986.

DWIGHT, ELEANOR. *Edith Wharton: An Extraordinary Life.* New York: Harry N. Abrams, 1999.

LAWSON, RICHARD. *Edith Wharton.* New York: Ungar Press, 1977.

MCDOWELL, MARGARET. *Edith Wharton.* Boston: Twayne Publishers, 1990.

SPRINGER, MARLENE. *Ethan Frome: A Nightmare of Need.* New York: Twayne Publishers, 1993.

WALTON, GEOFFREY. *Edith Wharton: A Critical Interpretation.* Rutherford, New Jersey: Fairleigh Dickinson University Press, 1982.

REVIEW & RESOURCES

SparkNotes Study Guides: